P9-DFX-624

Mini Bar *Vodka*

Mini Bar Vodka

by MITTIE HELLMICH

photographs by Laura Stojanovic

CHRONICLE BOOKS

SAN FRANCISCO

This 2008 boxed set edition published exclusively for Barnes & Noble, Inc., by Chronicle Books LLC.

Text copyright © 2006 by Mittie Hellmich. Photographs copyright © 2006 by Laura Stojanovic.
All rights reserved. No part of this book may be reproduced in any form without written
permission from the publisher.

Boxed set ISBN: 978-1-4351-0794-6

The Library of Congress has cataloged the previous edition as follows:
Hellmich, Mittie, 1960-
  Mini bar vodka / by Mittie Hellmich.
     p. cm.
  ISBN 978-0-8118-5321-7
  1. Cocktails. 2. Vodka. I. Title. II. Title: Vodka. III. Title: Mini bar vodka.
  TX951.H44847 2008
   641.2'5--dc22
  2008014805

Manufactured in China

Prop styling by Barbara Fierros
Food styling by William Smith
Designed by Hallie Overman, Brooklyn NY

10 9 8 7 6 5 4 3 2 1

Chronicle Books LLC
680 Second Street
San Francisco, California 94107
www.chroniclebooks.com

7-Up is a registered trademark of The Seven-Up Company. Baileys Original Irish Cream is a
registered trademark of R & A Bailey & Co., Limited. Cîroc is a registered trademark of Diageo North
America, Inc. Clamato is a registered trademark of Cbi Holdings, Inc. Cointreau is a registered
trademark of Cointreau Corporation. Frangelico is a registered trademark of C&C International Limited.
Galliano is a registered trademark of John Galliano S.A. Grand Marnier is a registered trademark
of Societe Des Produits Marnier-Lapostolle. Kahlúa is a registered trademark of The Kahlua Company.
Lillet is a registered trademark of Societe Lillet Freres. Mandarine Napoleon. Midori is a registered
trademark of Suntory Limited. Orangina is a registered trademark of Orangina Beverages, Inc. San
Pellegrino is a registered trademark of San Pellegrino S.P.A. Sex and the City is a registered
trademark of Time Warner Entertainment Company, L.P. Smirnoff is a registered trademark of Diageo
North America, Inc. Southern Comfort is a registered trademark of Southern Comfort Properties, Inc.
Suntory is a registered trademark of Suntory Limited. Tia Maria is a registered trademark of Tia Maria
Limited. Tuaca is a registered trademark of Distillerie Tuoni & Canepa S.P.A. Zubrowka Bison Vodka
is a registered trademark of Przedsiebiorstwo Polmos Bialystok S.A.

Table of Contents

EASY-TO-PREPARE COCKTAILS with four ingredients or less 14

Simple

ESSENTIAL RECIPES for every bartender 28

Savvy

A LITTLE MORE WORK but definitely worth the effort 46

Sophisticated

LUXURIOUS YUMMINESS for your mouth 60

Sensual

CAFFEINATED AND FIZZY DRINKS for a fun buzz 70

Stimulating

Introduction

THE MEANING OF THE WORD *VODKA* IN RUSSIAN—"LITTLE WATER"—PERFECTLY CHARACTERIZES THIS CLEAN AND MOST NEUTRAL OF ALL SPIRITS. WITH VIRTUALLY NO DISCERNIBLE FLAVOR OR AROMA, VODKA IS THE CHAMELEON OF LIQUORS, MELDING SEAMLESSLY INTO ANY MIXOLOGICAL CONCOCTION.

This crystal-clear spirit may be synonymous with the chilly northern and eastern European cultures of Scandinavia, Russia, Poland, and the Ukraine, but it was the alchemically inclined Italians who brought the art of distillation to the area. Northern Europeans, however, can take credit for distilling vodka to perfection. Ever since, they have consumed it like, well, water—as a bracer against the harsh northern winters and a potable balm to bolster the spirits. Although they say that the farther north the vodka hails from, the better it is, there are always exceptions. France has brought its refined palate into the vodka market with a few remarkable premium vodkas, including Ciroc, which is distilled from grapes.

Vodka is typically made from either potatoes or grains such as rye, wheat, corn, and barley. Most vodkas are distilled in continuous stills, where the spirit is heated, cooled, and then filtered to remove unwanted trace elements such as botanicals and minerals that would otherwise lend flavor and aroma. Some, however, are made in old-fashioned pot stills to retain a whisper of original flavor.

Vodka can be made from virtually any botanical substance, because once it has been distilled, the spirit is filtered through activated charcoal to remove any remaining impurities and harsh edges, resulting in a neutral, clean taste. Yet, even in highly filtered spirits, the original substance influences the outcome. For example, potatoes characteristically produce vodka with a creamy quality, whereas rye-based vodkas have a bite and wheat-based spirits a more subtle delicacy. Unlike other spirits (with the exception of a few Polish and Russian vodkas aged in oak), vodka achieves its mild smoothness through multiple filtrations rather than through aging, with the highest-quality vodkas filtered many times. Some producers go to the extreme with exotic methods using silver birch charcoal or pure quartz sand; Suhoi vodka is purportedly filtered through diamonds.

Vodka has become the top-selling spirit in American bars, but this wasn't always the case. Virtually unknown outside northern Europe until the late 1940s, vodka was introduced to these shores by a Russian refugee named Vladimir Smirnoff. Vodka distiller to the czar, Smirnoff escaped to America after the Bolshevik Revolution and introduced his new country to the specialty of his homeland. For decades the exotic spirit was vaguely linked to dark Chekhov plays and Tolstoy novels. But in 1946 the Moscow Mule propelled vodka into the mainstream. Made with vodka, lime, and ginger beer and served in a copper mug, the cocktail soon tripled Smirnoff's sales. By the 1960s, vodka was firmly entrenched in our cocktail repertoire with drinks like the Screwdriver and the Bloody Mary. It even infiltrated the hallowed realm of the Gin Martini once James Bond glamorized his signature Vodka Martini.

The essentially neutral character of vodka makes it the most ideal spirit for mixing in a wide variety of cocktails. When it comes to the many vodka styles available, the best choice for mixed drinks is the moderately priced Russian, Scandinavian, and American vodkas for their clean, tasteless quality. Premium vodkas, typically from eastern Europe or France, tend to have more discernible aromatic whispers and nuances of flavor, from citrus and sea spray to herbs, spices, or pepper. These spirits should be savored, so reserve your high-end vodkas for icy shots, Martinis, and Vodka Tonics. The most distinctive feature of vodka, often taken for granted, is its "mouthfeel," or how it feels in the mouth and on the palate. Whether the texture is oily or soft, viscous or buttery, it is all part of the vodka experience.

With the exception of an elite group of Vodka Martini fans, Americans are an eccentric lot, preferring to mix their vodka in a variety of cocktails. Russians, Poles, Swedes, and western Europeans still enjoy their vodka neat, either as an aperitif before a meal or sipped as an after-dinner drink.

Key to enjoying vodka for vodka's sake is to chill it in the freezer, not only to enhance the flavor but also to promote its viscosity. The traditional ritual of serving vodka straight from the freezer neat, in a small glass, is the best way to savor a great vodka. Although some enjoy it over ice, many purists find such a practice sacrilegious, as the vodka becomes too diluted. However, sipping anything less than a superpremium vodka will deliver a somewhat harsh finish sure to evoke Dostoyevskian angst.

The new darling of contemporary mixology may be flavored vodkas, but the techniques used to make them date back to the eleventh and twelfth centuries, when Polish and Russian households began adding herbs, spices, and fruits to vodka to help mask the harsh taste of rudimentary distillates. Today there's an ever-widening selection of mouthwatering flavored vodkas on the market, from lemon and orange to raspberry, mandarin, grapefruit, peach, chocolate, black currant, apple, pepper, cranberry, and vanilla—not to mention easily homemade infusions with personalized botanical combinations. They have opened up a whole new world of creative options, adding an extra flavor dimension to cocktails.

So, before the clinking of glasses and the toasting starts, consider the possibilities beyond traditional shots of vodka. This little book will lead you into the world of the Cosmopolitan and the Lemon Drop, inviting you to shake or stir your way through a fabulous collection of swank and sophisticated cocktails, refreshingly fizzy coolers, and luxuriously creamy nightcaps, all made with enticing ingredients that embrace vodka in all its versatile glory.

Za vashe zdorovye! (To your health!)

Glassware, Tools, and Terminology

Glassware plays an important role in the much-ritualized cocktail experience. A well-chilled vessel visually entices us with the promise of refreshment, with the right glass adding elegance to even the simplest drink. Glasses come in an endless variety of designs, styles, and colors, but when it comes to setting up your home bar, your repertoire of glassware doesn't have to be extensive to be stylishly appropriate and proficiently functional. A few basic styles— cocktail glasses, highball glasses, old-fashioned and double old-fashioned glasses, champagne flutes, and wineglasses— will see you beautifully through a multitude of drinks.

ESSENTIAL BAR TOOLS

Whether you have a swank bar setup in your favorite entertaining room or an area set aside in the kitchen, you don't need all the high-tech gadgets and gizmos to put together a well-functioning home bar. All you need are the essential bar tools to see you through just about any mixological occasion. You may already have the typical kitchen tools you need: a sharp paring knife for cutting fruit and garnishes, a cutting board for cutting fruit, a bar towel, a good corkscrew and bottle opener, and measuring spoons and cups. To these you will want to add a few of the basic bar tools: a blender with a high-caliber motor, a citrus juicer, a cocktail shaker or a mixing pitcher and stirring rod, a bar spoon, a jigger, an ice bucket and tongs, and, of course, a few cocktail picks and swizzle sticks.

To dash, muddle, top, or float: That is the question. When you want clarification on what exactly that all means or what it means to have a drink served up, neat, straight, or on the rocks, this miniglossary of frequently used bar terms will assist you in navigating bar talk.

· Chaser · The beverage you drink immediately after you have downed anything alcoholic, usually a shot. Typical chasers are beer, club soda, and juice.

· Dash · Either a shake from a bitters bottle or the equivalent of approximately ⅛ teaspoon.

· Dry · A term meaning "not sweet," used either in reference to some wines or to describe nonsweet spirits or cocktails, such as the Dry Martini, which uses dry vermouth rather than sweet vermouth.

· Float · This describes the technique of slowly pouring a small amount of spirit (usually a liqueur or cream) over the surface of a drink so that it floats, or sits atop another liquid without mixing. The customary technique is to slowly pour the liquid over the back of a spoon.

· Highball · The main characteristics of a highball drink are that it has two ingredients—one spirit and one mixer, usually carbonated, poured into a tall, narrow glass filled with ice (the shape of the glass helps to contain the carbonation)—and that it can be mixed very quickly.

· Lowball · A lowball is any drink served with ice in a short glass such as an old-fashioned glass.

· Muddle · A technique that involves using a small wooden "muddler" or spoon to mash fruits or herbs in the bottom of the glass, usually together with bitters or sugar, to release their aromatic flavors.

· Neat · Describes a single spirit or liqueur served in a glass "straight up"—enjoyed on its own, unchilled, and without ice, water, or any other ingredients.

· Neutral Spirit · A spirit distilled from grain to produce a virtually tasteless, colorless alcohol that is 95.5 percent ABV (alcohol by volume) and is used as a base for spirits such as vodka or gin or for blending with straight whiskeys or other spirits and liqueurs.

· On the Rocks · A term used to describe any liquor or mixed drink served over ice—the "rocks" being ice cubes— as opposed to a drink served "up" (without ice).

· Perfect · A term used to describe specific cocktails that contain equal parts dry and sweet vermouth, as in a Perfect Manhattan or Perfect Martini.

· Pousse-Café · Literally translated as the "coffee-pusher" (and pronounced poos-caf-FAY), this after-dinner drink layers colorful strata of liqueurs, syrups, spirits, and creams in a stemmed glass. The multiple layers—as many as seven—are artfully floated one on top of another so that each stratum remains separate. The heaviest liquid goes in first, the lightest is added last.

· Proof · A legal measurement of the alcoholic strength of a spirit. In the United States, proof is calculated thusly:

1 degree of proof equals 0.5 percent ABV (alcohol by volume). Therefore, a spirit labeled "80 proof" is 40 percent ABV, a 100-proof spirit is 50 percent ABV, and so on.

· Splash · A small amount that can fall anywhere between a dash and about an ounce, depending on who's doing the splashing.

· Straight · This term describes a spirit served without any other liquor or mixers, either poured into a chilled glass or over ice, occasionally with the addition of a splash of club soda or water.

· Top or Top Off · A term used by bartenders to describe the act of pouring the last ingredient into a drink, usually club soda or ginger ale, filling to the top of the glass. Also used to describe filling a beer mug from a tap.

· Up · Describes a drink served without ice in a cocktail glass. Usually the drink is shaken in a cocktail shaker and strained "up" into a chilled cocktail glass, as opposed to "on the rocks," which means served over ice.

simple

· Easy-to-prepare cocktails with four ingredients or less ·

Bay Breeze

AHH ... CRANBERRY JUICE, the quintessential ingredient that conjures up salty Atlantic sea breezes when it shows up in drinks such as the Cape Codder and the Madras. However, when paired up with its Caribbean soulmate pineapple juice, cranberry juice and vodka transform into one tall, tropical summer refresher.

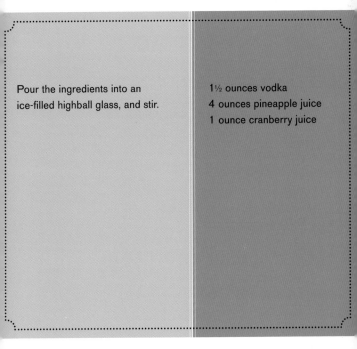

Pour the ingredients into an ice-filled highball glass, and stir.

1½ ounces vodka
4 ounces pineapple juice
1 ounce cranberry juice

Cape Codder

THIS CLASSIC DRINK HAS MANY LOYALISTS, and for good reason—you just cannot beat the sweet-tartness of cranberry juice combined with zingy lime for a reliably great thirst-quencher. This fabulously perfected flavor combo also helps make the Cosmopolitan so good.

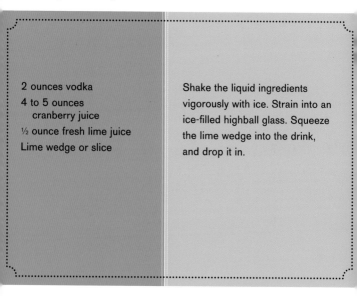

2 ounces vodka

4 to 5 ounces
   cranberry juice

½ ounce fresh lime juice

Lime wedge or slice

Shake the liquid ingredients vigorously with ice. Strain into an ice-filled highball glass. Squeeze the lime wedge into the drink, and drop it in.

· Variations · For a bit of effervescence, add a splash of club soda.

For a CLASSIC MADRAS, add 2 ounces orange juice and top with the cranberry juice, slowly blending; do not stir.

Goldfinger

THIS SWINGING LIBATION IS THE PERFECT SNAPSHOT OF 1970s
POP CULTURE—a shimmering golden cocktail that simultaneously
symbolized the stylish James Bond movie and spotlighted
Galliano, the new Italian liqueur on the scene. Modernist in its
simplicity yet lush, this little number elevates the swank
factor, with the sweet anise tones of Galliano whispering through
the pineapple juice.

Shake the ingredients vigorously
with ice. Strain into a chilled
cocktail glass.

1½ ounces vodka
¾ ounce Galliano
1 ounce pineapple juice

Greyhound

FOR THOSE WHO ADORE GRAPEFRUIT JUICE, this suburban classic is a refreshingly tart spin-off of the Screwdriver. Made as originally intended, with fresh-squeezed grapefruit juice instead of the subpar canned juice that is used all too frequently, the Greyhound is sublime in its simplicity. For a slightly sweeter version, try using fresh-squeezed Ruby Red grapefruit juice. And for a touch of sweet orange flavor to take the edge off the grapefruit bite, add 1 ounce Grand Marnier, shaking the drink and serving it in a cocktail glass.

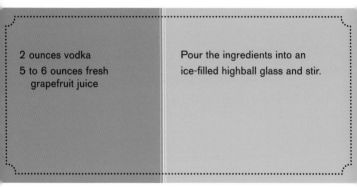

2 ounces vodka

5 to 6 ounces fresh
grapefruit juice

Pour the ingredients into an ice-filled highball glass and stir.

· Variations · For a SALTY DOG, serve in a highball glass rimmed with a lemon wedge and then kosher salt.

For a LEMON DOG, substitute citron vodka for the regular vodka.

Screwdriver

AS COCKTAIL LEGEND TELLS IT, THIS CLASSIC 1950S HIGHBALL got its name from American oilmen working on a rig in Iran— they used their screwdrivers as stir sticks to blend vodka and orange juice. The drink caught on, despite the stirring implement, and quickly became a favorite Sunday brunch libation. Make it with fresh orange juice for optimum enjoyment.

Pour the vodka and orange juice into an ice-filled highball glass, and stir. Garnish with the orange slice.

2 ounces vodka
4 to 6 ounces fresh
    orange juice
Orange slice

· Variations · For a SLOW COMFORTABLE SCREW, add ½ ounce sloe gin and ½ ounce Southern Comfort.

For a CORDLESS SCREWDRIVER, serve chilled vodka in a shot glass, accompanied with an orange slice dipped in sugar. Gulp down the vodka, and then bite into the orange slice.

Russian Quaalude

THE ONLY THING RUSSIAN ABOUT THIS DRINK may be the vodka, but its Italian hazelnut and Irish coffee–tinged whiskey flavors are sure to send you on a creamy, dreamy international trip. This drink can also be served as a layered pousse-café by carefully pouring in the ingredients in the order given.

¾ ounce Frangelico
¾ ounce Irish cream liqueur
¾ ounce vodka

Shake the ingredients vigorously with ice. Strain into a chilled cocktail glass or into an ice-filled old-fashioned glass.

Vodka Tonic

THIS CLEAR, SPARKLING COOLER is the perfect summer drink for those who also prefer their Martinis made with vodka instead of gin. The proportional balance of vodka to tonic is indeed a personal call, but a couple extra wedges of lime are a well-deserved bonus on a hot, humid day.

1 to 3 lime wedges
2 ounces vodka
3 to 5 ounces chilled
   tonic water

Rim a chilled highball glass with a lime wedge, and drop it in. Fill the glass with ice, pour in the vodka, and top with tonic water. Squeeze the remaining lime wedges into the drink, and drop them in.

Suntory Cocktail

THIS COCKTAIL IS NAMED AFTER THE JAPANESE DISTILLERY that produces Midori. The popular muskmelon-flavored liqueur lends its glowing chartreuse hue to this citrusy Martini.

Shake the ingredients vigorously with ice. Strain into a chilled cocktail glass.

- 1½ ounces lemon-flavored vodka
- 1 ounce Midori or other melon-flavored liqueur
- 1 ounce fresh grapefruit juice

Pearl Harbor

THIS PACIFIC RIM COCKTAIL brings together the sweet, delicate muskmelon flavors of Midori and pineapple juice in a much more harmonious fusion of Oriental and Occidental than history would suggest. Midori is the most familiar of the melon liqueurs.

Shake the ingredients vigorously with ice. Strain into a chilled cocktail glass.

- 1½ ounces vodka
- ¾ ounce Midori or other melon-flavored liqueur
- 1 ounce pineapple juice

Watermelon

SUMMERTIME, AND THE LIVING IS BREEZY—especially when you add an exotic splash of fruity melon liqueur to the eastern seaboard's favorite cran-vodka combo.

Shake the ingredients with ice.
Strain into an ice-filled collins glass.

1 ounce vodka
1 ounce melon-flavored liqueur
2 ounces cranberry juice
Dash of grenadine

Woo Woo

THERE MUST HAVE BEEN SOMETHING IN THE WATER in the 1970s that promoted an uncontrollable urge to splash peach schnapps into every concoction. This drink did not escape the craze, losing the Cape Coddesque lime for the peachy sweet schnapps.

Shake the ingredients with ice. Strain into an ice-filled highball glass.

1¼ ounces vodka
¾ ounce peach schnapps
3 ounces cranberry juice

savvy

· Essential recipes for every bartender ·

Moscow Mule

THIS IS THE DRINK THAT USHERED VODKA INTO THE MAINSTREAM.
The effervescent, zippy classic 1940s recipe, its defining touch a
brilliant squeeze of lime, was concocted by Smirnoff rep John
Martin and Jack Morgan, owner of the Cock 'n' Bull Restaurant
in Hollywood, to promote the not-yet-popular Russian spirit.
The original drink was served in a copper mug engraved with
kicking mules, but a collins glass is perfectly acceptable. A
milder Moscow Mule can be made with ginger ale instead of the
traditional spicy ginger beer. For an exotic twist, try the Vespa
cocktail, which replaces 1 ounce banana liqueur for the
lime juice—or even better yet, combines it with the lime juice.

Pour the vodka and lime juice into
an ice-filled highball glass. Top with
ginger beer and stir. Squeeze the
lime wedge into the drink, and drop
it in.

2 ounces vodka
½ ounce fresh lime juice
4 ounces ginger beer
    or ginger ale
Lime wedge

Bloody Mary

THIS CLASSIC AMERICAN COCKTAIL that's as much a weekend tradition as the ritualistic reading of the Sunday paper, actually originated in Paris in the mid-1920s, at Harry's New York Bar. It landed in Manhattan in 1934 along with its creator, bartender Fernand "Pete" Petiot, who came to tend bar at the King Cole Bar in the St. Regis Hotel. Vodka wasn't available in the United States at the time, so he was forced to improvise with gin, and called it the less offensive "Red Snapper." The original cocktail was a much simpler, and blander, blend of vodka and tomato juice. Not surprisingly, New Yorkers found the drink quite dull, and requested a spicier version, spurring the creation we enjoy today. Hemingway further popularized it as a favorite hangover remedy.

Shake the liquid ingredients and horseradish vigorously with ice. Strain into an ice-filled highball glass. Squeeze the lemon wedge over the drink, and drop it in. Garnish with the celery stick.

2 ounces vodka

4 ounces tomato juice

½ ounce fresh lemon juice

2 to 3 dashes Tabasco sauce

2 to 3 dashes Worcestershire sauce

¼ teaspoon horseradish (freshly grated, if possible)

Lemon wedge

Celery stick

· Variations on the Bloody Mary · For a south-of-the-border version, use extra-tart lime juice instead of the traditional lemon, and use pepper-infused vodka to really push the hot-and-spicy factor.

For a BLOODY MARY DELUXE, top with chilled champagne.

For a CAESAR (also known as a BLOODY CAESAR or CLAMDIGGER), substitute Clamato juice for the tomato juice.

For a BLOODY MARIE, add ½ teaspoon anisette.

For a VIRGIN MARY, simply omit the vodka.

Sea Breeze

YET ANOTHER THIRST-QUENCHING SUMMER CLASSIC built upon cranberry juice, with the addition of grapefruit juice to really tart things up.

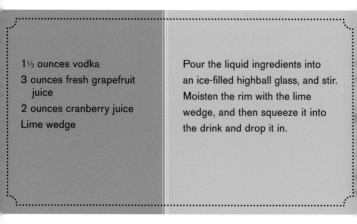

1½ ounces vodka
3 ounces fresh grapefruit
   juice
2 ounces cranberry juice
Lime wedge

Pour the liquid ingredients into an ice-filled highball glass, and stir. Moisten the rim with the lime wedge, and then squeeze it into the drink and drop it in.

Harvey Wallbanger

THIS 1970s CLASSIC comes with a very dubious, but entertaining tale surrounding its conception (some suspect the producer of Galliano of inventing the story). In the 1960s, a California surfer named—that's right—Harvey was determinedly consoling himself after a lost surfing contest. He decided a splash of Galliano in his screwdriver would be the perfect antidote. After a few of these, he was careening into walls and furniture, earning himself the nickname "Wallbanger," as did his concoction. Whatever the story, a float of Galliano is indeed a fabulous improvement on the basic Screwdriver.

Shake the vodka and orange juice with ice, and strain into an ice-filled highball glass. Float the Galliano on top of the drink.

1½ ounces vodka
4 to 5 ounces fresh orange juice
½ ounce Galliano

Original Cosmopolitan

THIS WILDLY POPULAR COCKTAIL, created in the late 1980s, became the darling of the *Sex and the City* set and now reigns as a stylish urban classic. The original recipe, concocted by Toby Cecchini at the Odeon Bar in New York, is a perfectly proportioned balance of citron vodka, tart lime juice, Cointreau for a little sweetness, and enough cranberry juice to lend a slight blush. The original has a well-crafted integrity not found in the cranberry-heavy transmutations most Cosmos have evolved into. For those who do prefer more cranberry flavor, add 1 ounce cranberry juice, and for cranberry nuts, see the Crantini variation (page 36).

Shake the liquid ingredients vigorously with ice. Strain into a chilled cocktail glass. Garnish with the lemon peel twist.

1½ ounces citron vodka
1½ ounces Cointreau
1 ounce fresh lime juice
1 to 2 dashes cranberry juice
Lemon peel twist

· Variations on the Cosmopolitan · For a MANDARIN COSMO, substitute mandarin vodka for the citron and Mandarine Napoléon liqueur for the Cointreau, then add a splash of mandarin orange juice.

For those who refuse to be seen holding a pink drink, there is the WHITE COSMO, made with white cranberry juice instead of the regular.

For a METROPOLITAN, replace the citron vodka with black currant vodka and garnish with a slice of lime.

For a GINGER COSMO, add a few thin slices of fresh ginger and shake with the liquid ingredients.

For a CRANTINI, substitute cranberry-flavored vodka for the citron vodka, add 1 ounce of cranberry juice, and reduce the lime juice to ½ ounce.

Lemon Drop

THIS DELECTABLE NEW CLASSIC is one of those deceivingly candy-esque cocktails that has the perfect balance of sweet and tart—and a potency that definitely warrants moderation. I recommend putting the vodka in the freezer for a couple hours until it is icy cold to further improve this refreshing cocktail. For a Bullfrog, pour the shaken ingredients into an ice-filled highball glass, top with club soda, and squeeze a wedge of lemon into the drink.

Rub the rim of a chilled large cocktail glass with the lemon wedge, and rim with sugar. Shake the liquid ingredients vigorously with ice. Strain into the prepared glass. Garnish with the lemon peel twist.

Lemon wedge

Superfine sugar

1½ ounces lemon-flavored vodka

1 ounce Grand Marnier or Cointreau

1½ ounces fresh lemon juice

½ ounce fresh orange juice

Lemon peel twist

Melon Ball

MIDORI, THAT VIBRANT CHARTREUSE-HUED, MUSKMELON-FLAVORED LIQUEUR, adds a complex kick to the classic Screwdriver.

Shake the liquid ingredients vigorously with ice. Strain into an ice-filled wineglass. Garnish with the orange slice and watermelon wedge.

1 ounce vodka
1 ounce Midori or other melon-flavored liqueur
4 ounces fresh orange juice
Orange slice
Watermelon wedge

Belmont Stakes

THE SIGNATURE DRINK SERVED AT THE BELMONT STAKES HORSE RACE is one smooth cocktail just potent enough to fuel a day of reckless betting.

Shake the liquid ingredients vigorously with ice. Strain into a chilled cocktail glass. Garnish with the orange slice.

1½ ounces vodka
½ ounce gold rum
½ ounce strawberry liqueur
Dash of grenadine
½ ounce fresh lime juice
Orange slice

Ballet Russe

THIS DRINK IS AS PRETTY AS A TUTU, and the blush of pink hides one zingy little cocktail. In the mood for something tall and fizzy? Strain it over ice in a highball glass and top with ginger ale to make an effervescent Russian Fizz.

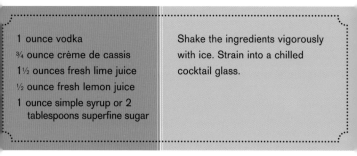

1 ounce vodka
¾ ounce crème de cassis
1½ ounces fresh lime juice
½ ounce fresh lemon juice
1 ounce simple syrup or 2
    tablespoons superfine sugar

Shake the ingredients vigorously with ice. Strain into a chilled cocktail glass.

· Basic Simple Syrup · Also known as SUGAR SYRUP, this is an essential ingredient in many drinks, as it requires no dissolving or excessive stirring to incorporate, unlike granulated sugar. When stored in a clean, covered jar and refrigerated, the syrup will keep indefinitely. Makes 2 cups.

1 cup water   2 cups sugar

In a small saucepan, bring the water to a boil. Remove the pan from the heat and add the sugar. Stir until the sugar is completely dissolved. Cool completely before using or refrigerating. Pour into a clean glass jar, cap tightly, and store in the refrigerator until needed.

Kamikaze Cocktail

SOME MAY CONSIDER THE KAMIKAZE A VODKA SHOOTER DRINK, but the cocktail version, made with Cointreau and served up in a frosty martini glass, is a much more refined way to go.

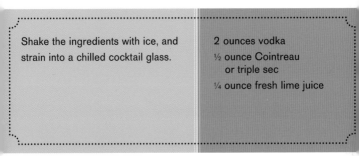

Shake the ingredients with ice, and strain into a chilled cocktail glass.

2 ounces vodka
½ ounce Cointreau or triple sec
¼ ounce fresh lime juice

Vodka Gimlet

THIS VODKA VERSION OF THE CLASSIC GIN-BASED GIMLET uses the original 50-50 ratio of lime juice to liquor and is made with the signature Gimlet ingredient—Rose's lime juice. Use only ½ ounce of Rose's for a drier, more modern drink.

Stir the ingredients in a mixing glass with ice. Strain into a chilled cocktail glass.

1½ ounces vodka
1½ ounces Rose's lime juice

Vodka Martini

THIS CLEAR, SHIMMERING COCKTAIL, otherwise known as the vodkatini, surpassed the traditional Gin Martini in popularity by the late 1950s and became a stylish staple in America's suburban dens. Vodka Martini drinkers tend to concur with James Bond, who not only promoted the preference for Russian vodka into mainstream cocktail culture, but also the shaken, not stirred, method.

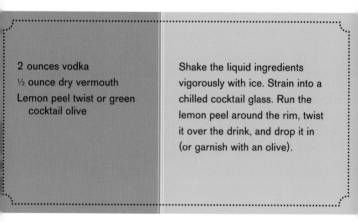

2 ounces vodka
½ ounce dry vermouth
Lemon peel twist or green cocktail olive

Shake the liquid ingredients vigorously with ice. Strain into a chilled cocktail glass. Run the lemon peel around the rim, twist it over the drink, and drop it in (or garnish with an olive).

· Variations · For a KANGAROO, use 1½ ounces vodka and ¾ ounce dry vermouth.

For a DIRTY VODKA MARTINI, add a dash of juice from a jar of green olives.

For a "BONE-DRY" VODKA MARTINI, simply sip chilled vodka neat.

White Russian

AT THE END OF THE EVENING, this rich and creamy coffee-flavored classic is the ultimate answer to dessert cravings. White Russians can be enjoyed served over ice, elegantly up, or as a frothy blended drink.

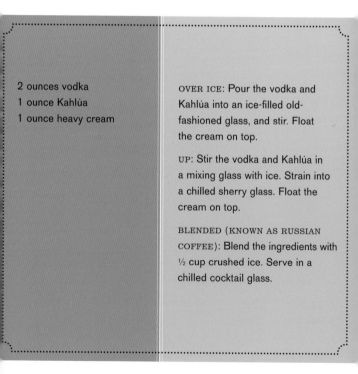

2 ounces vodka

1 ounce Kahlúa

1 ounce heavy cream

OVER ICE: Pour the vodka and Kahlúa into an ice-filled old-fashioned glass, and stir. Float the cream on top.

UP: Stir the vodka and Kahlúa in a mixing glass with ice. Strain into a chilled sherry glass. Float the cream on top.

BLENDED (KNOWN AS RUSSIAN COFFEE): Blend the ingredients with ½ cup crushed ice. Serve in a chilled cocktail glass.

White Spider

THIS VODKA VARIATION ON THE CLASSIC STINGER is the quintessential nightcap, with many versions varying according to personal taste. Peppermint schnapps is preferred over the usual crème de menthe, and while some prefer this drink up, others enjoy it "misting" over crushed ice.

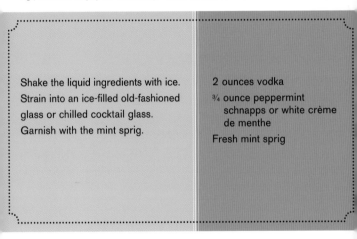

Shake the liquid ingredients with ice. Strain into an ice-filled old-fashioned glass or chilled cocktail glass. Garnish with the mint sprig.

2 ounces vodka
¾ ounce peppermint schnapps or white crème de menthe
Fresh mint sprig

· Variations · For a MINT MARTINI, increase the peppermint schnapps to 1¼ ounces, and serve in a chilled cocktail glass.

For a GREEN RUSSIAN, substitute green crème de menthe for the peppermint schnapps.

For a GREEN SPIDER, substitute green crème de menthe for the peppermint schnapps, and add a splash of tonic water.

· sophisticated ·

· A little more work but definitely worth the effort ·

Pomegranate Martini

POMEGRANATE JUICE IS THE NEW EXOTIC LIQUID on the cocktail scene, showing up in many a concoction. But like many things, what's old is new again, given that classic grenadine is simply pomegranate syrup. Not only is this drink a deep red, refreshingly tart alternative to the cranberry-based Cosmo, it has the bonus of being packed full of antioxidants. You can find pomegranate juice in well-stocked supermarkets and natural foods stores.

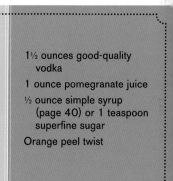

In a cocktail shaker, shake all the ingredients but the garnish vigorously with ice. Strain into a chilled cocktail glass. Garnish with the orange peel twist.

1½ ounces good-quality vodka
1 ounce pomegranate juice
½ ounce simple syrup (page 40) or 1 teaspoon superfine sugar
Orange peel twist

· Variations · For a minimalist approach, replace the pomegranate juice with ¼ cup fresh pomegranate seeds.

For a POMINTINI, add 2 fresh mint leaves, and shake with the other ingredients.

Apple Martini

A NEW ADDITION TO THE FLAVORED MARTINI CRAZE, this cocktail was purportedly first served at Lola's in Los Angeles, where it was called the Adam's Apple Martini, named after the bartender. Desired for its sweet yet puckery over-the-top apple flavor, the drink is technically not a Martini at all—but we won't bother with semantics when it tastes this good. For a real souped-up version, replace the regular vodka with Zubrowka Bison grass vodka, and add ¼ ounce butterscotch schnapps.

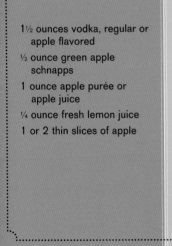

1½ ounces vodka, regular or apple flavored

½ ounce green apple schnapps

1 ounce apple purée or apple juice

¼ ounce fresh lemon juice

1 or 2 thin slices of apple

Shake the liquid ingredients vigorously with ice. Strain into a chilled cocktail glass. Garnish with the apple slices.

Pearl Diver Martini

INSPIRED BY THE LOVE OF FRESH GINGER, I found a great way
to infuse this Saketini with an abundance of pan-Asian flavor.
Simply adding ¼ cup thinly sliced fresh ginger to a 750-ml
bottle of your favorite vodka and steeping the concoction for
a day or two will yield a spicy, ginger-infused vodka to float
your sake upon.

Stir the vodka in a mixing glass
with ice. Strain into a chilled glass.
Slowly pour the sake to float on
top of the drink. Garnish with the
orange peel twist or candied ginger.

2 ounces ginger-
  infused vodka

½ ounce chilled
  premium sake

Orange peel twist or thin
  slice of candied ginger

Caipirovska

MOSCOW MEETS RIO IN THIS THIRST-QUENCHING DRINK inspired by the Caipirinha. Made with vodka instead of the traditional cachaça, it makes for a great alternative to the basic Vodka Tonic, especially when it's enjoyed with a splash of club soda. For an Orange Caipirovska, substitute orange or mandarin vodka for the regular vodka and a few orange and lemon wedges for the lime.

Muddle the lime with the sugar in the bottom of an old-fashioned glass. Fill the glass with crushed ice, add the vodka, and stir well.

1 lime, cut into 8 wedges
1 tablespoon sugar
2 ounces vodka

Orange Martini

A WELL-BALANCED MELDING of Lillet—an aromatized wine with delicate notes of honey, citrus, and mint—with fragrant orange flower water makes this cocktail a unique libation.

Orange wedge
Superfine sugar
3 ounces orange-flavored vodka
¼ ounce Lillet Blanc
Drop of orange flower water
Orange peel twist

Rub the rim of a chilled cocktail glass with the orange wedge, and rim with sugar. Stir the liquid ingredients with ice in a mixing glass. Strain into the prepared glass. Garnish with the orange peel twist.

Tokyo Mary

FOR WASABI AND GINGER FANATICS, this variation on the Bloody Mary is a fabulous alternative with an extra-spicy Asian twist—so packed with savory flavors that you might just find you can't go back to the traditional version.

Rub the rim of a chilled highball glass with the lime wedge. Combine the wasabi, garlic, ginger, soy sauce, lemon juice, and pepper in the bottom of the glass. Fill the glass with ice, add the vodka and tomato juice, and stir. Squeeze the lime wedge into the drink, and drop it in. Garnish with the lemongrass stalk for a stir stick.

Lime wedge

½ teaspoon wasabi paste or prepared horseradish

½ teaspoon minced garlic

¼ teaspoon grated fresh ginger

4 dashes soy sauce

½ ounce fresh lemon juice

Pinch of freshly cracked pepper

2 ounces vodka, regular or pepper-flavored

3 ounces chilled tomato juice

Lemongrass stalk

Pink Lemonade

THIS ADULT VERSION OF THE KIDDIE JUICE BOX tastes so deceivingly innocent and goes down sooo easy that it has a way of sneaking up on you.

1½ ounces vodka
½ ounce triple sec
1 ounce cranberry juice
½ ounce fresh lemon juice
½ ounce fresh lime juice
4 to 5 ounces chilled 7-Up
Lemon wedge

Shake all the liquid ingredients except the 7-Up vigorously with ice. Strain into an ice-filled collins glass. Top with 7-Up, and stir gently. Squeeze the lemon wedge over the drink, and drop it in.

Ruby Martini

CRANBERRY JUICE AND ORANGE-FLAVORED, AQUA-HUED BLUE CURAÇAO COME TOGETHER for a shimmering crimson gem of a cocktail.

1½ ounces vodka
½ ounce blue curaçao
½ ounce cranberry juice
Lemon peel twist

Stir the liquid ingredients in a mixing glass with ice. Strain into a chilled cocktail glass. Run the lemon peel around the rim, twist it over the drink, and drop it in.

Brass Monkey

BACK IN THE LATE 1960s, bartenders were turning basic drinks into exciting cocktails by merely floating Galliano's licorice-vanilla flavor on top. This classic has the added tropical velocity of rum.

1 ounce vodka
¾ ounce light rum
4 ounces fresh orange juice
½ ounce Galliano

Pour the vodka, rum, and orange juice into an ice-filled highball glass. Stir well. Float the Galliano on top.

Yellow Fever

I'M NOT SURE WHERE THE VISUALLY DESCRIPTIVE NAME OF THIS COCKTAIL ORIGINATED, but the Yellow Fever is so damn good it deserves a more evocative title—say, Amalfi Barfly?

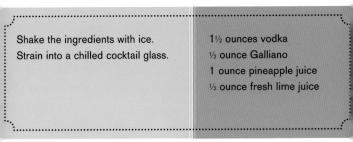

Shake the ingredients with ice. Strain into a chilled cocktail glass.

1½ ounces vodka
½ ounce Galliano
1 ounce pineapple juice
½ ounce fresh lime juice

Nutty Martini

YOU DON'T HAVE TO BE A FRANGELICO NUT to enjoy this elegantly minimal Martini. It does, however, deliver more than a hint of hazelnut—which must surely be sanctioned by the monks.

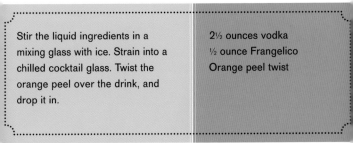

Stir the liquid ingredients in a mixing glass with ice. Strain into a chilled cocktail glass. Twist the orange peel over the drink, and drop it in.

2½ ounces vodka
½ ounce Frangelico
Orange peel twist

Sake Martini

A FLOAT OF HEADY PLUM WINE naturally complements the sake in this stylishly sublime Martini.

Stir the vodka and sake in a mixing glass with ice. Strain into a chilled cocktail glass. Float the plum wine on top of the drink.

2 ounces vodka
½ ounce dry sake
1 teaspoon plum wine

Agent Orange

DIG ORANGES? this is definitely the drink for you. Infused with rich brandy-based orange liqueurs and juiced up with fresh orange juice, this sunny cocktail is packed with a decadent profusion of aromatic orange flavors.

Shake the liquid ingredients vigorously with ice. Strain into a chilled cocktail glass. Run the orange peel around the rim, twist it over the drink, and drop it in.

1½ ounces vodka
¾ ounce Grand Marnier
¼ ounce Cointreau
½ ounce fresh orange juice
Orange peel twist

sensual

· Luxurious yumminess for your mouth ·

Chocolate Martini

A CHOCOHOLIC'S DREAM DRINK. You just can't get any more decadent than this luscious version of the Chocolatini, especially when you replace the usual brown crème de cacao with Godiva chocolate liqueur and dust the rim with cocoa powder.

Rub the rim of a chilled cocktail glass with the orange wedge, and rim with cocoa powder. Shake the liquid ingredients vigorously with ice. Strain into the prepared glass. Sprinkle the top of the drink with bittersweet chocolate shavings.

Orange wedge

Cocoa powder

1½ ounces vodka, regular or vanilla-flavored

¼ ounce Godiva chocolate liqueur or dark crème de cacao

¼ ounce white crème de cacao

Bittersweet chocolate shavings

· Variations on the Chocolate Martini · For a CLEAR CHOCOLATE MARTINI, substitute white crème de cacao for the Godiva.

For a WHITE CHOCOLATE MARTINI, rim the glass with powdered sugar, substitute Godiva White Chocolate Liqueur for the Godiva, and add ¼ ounce crème de banane. Garnish with white chocolate truffle shavings.

For a CHOCOLATE MANDARIN MARTINI, use mandarin-flavored vodka, and add ¼ ounce Mandarine Napoléon liqueur.

Purple Passion

IT'S MUCH TOO EASY TO FALL FOR THIS VIOLET-HUED LIBATION, which is intensely flavored with tart citrus and sweet grape juice. If you feel you can't be seen with a purple drink in your hand, there's always white grape juice to save your rep.

2 ounces vodka

3 ounces chilled purple grape juice

3 ounces fresh grapefruit juice

Pour the ingredients over ice in a chilled collins glass, and stir.

Love Potion

L'AMOUR IN A GLASS. Just a splash of Chambord—that lush, sweet French liqueur made by infusing Cognac with black raspberries, currants, blackberries, and red raspberries—is all you'll need to become completely infatuated with this ruby red jewel.

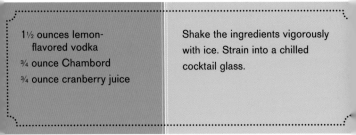

1½ ounces lemon-
    flavored vodka
¾ ounce Chambord
¾ ounce cranberry juice

Shake the ingredients vigorously with ice. Strain into a chilled cocktail glass.

Black Russian

THIS COLD WAR CLASSIC was created by bartender Gustave Tops, at the Hotel Metropole in Brussels around 1950. It eventually reached America and is now an after-dinner favorite.

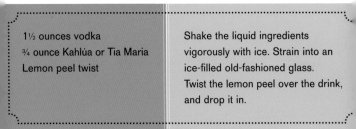

1½ ounces vodka
¾ ounce Kahlúa or Tia Maria
Lemon peel twist

Shake the liquid ingredients vigorously with ice. Strain into an ice-filled old-fashioned glass. Twist the lemon peel over the drink, and drop it in.

Pink Fetish

CRANBERRY, ORANGE, AND PEACH ARE A SEDUCTIVE TRIO of flavors that is irresistibly luscious. Add the zing of lime juice to counterbalance their sweetness, and you have one dangerously smooth cocktail to obsess over.

Shake the liquid ingredients vigorously with ice. Strain into an ice-filled old-fashioned glass. Squeeze the lime wedge into the drink, and drop it in.

1 ounce vodka
1 ounce peach schnapps
2 ounces cranberry juice
2 ounces fresh orange juice
Lime wedge

White Cloud

THIS COMPLETELY DECADENT COMBINATION of chocolate and tropical pineapple is sure to give you a bliss-filled, sunny disposition.

Shake the ingredients vigorously with ice. Strain into an ice-filled highball glass.

1½ ounces vodka
¾ ounce white crème de cacao
2 ounces pineapple juice
¾ ounce cream

Sex on the Beach #1

SEX ON THE BEACH ISN'T JUST A COCKTAIL, it represents an entire genre of drinks promising romantic interludes via liquid libations. Concocted for the swinging set, this sexual innuendo of a drink has spun off many different versions under the same catchy name. This version is an elaboration on the Sea Breeze (for another variation, simply add 3 ounces fresh orange juice).

Pour all the liquid ingredients into an ice-filled highball glass. Stir and garnish with the cherry.

1 ounce vodka
1 ounce peach schnapps
3 ounces cranberry juice
3 ounces fresh grapefruit juice
Maraschino cherry

Sex on the Beach #2

THIS VERSION TAKES A TROPICAL EXCURSION and is served up for a more elegant approach.

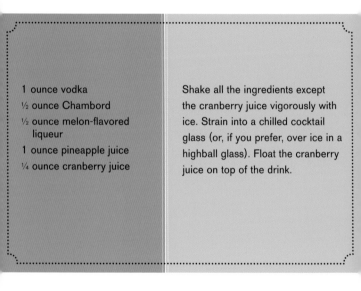

- 1 ounce vodka
- ½ ounce Chambord
- ½ ounce melon-flavored liqueur
- 1 ounce pineapple juice
- ¼ ounce cranberry juice

Shake all the ingredients except the cranberry juice vigorously with ice. Strain into a chilled cocktail glass (or, if you prefer, over ice in a highball glass). Float the cranberry juice on top of the drink.

Russian Bear

THE RUSSIAN BEAR IS KNOWN IN SOME CIRCLES AS A VELVET HAMMER, which should give you a clue as to just how smooth, creamy, and sweet this delectable little number is.

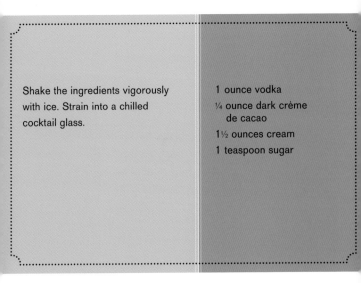

Shake the ingredients vigorously with ice. Strain into a chilled cocktail glass.

1 ounce vodka
¼ ounce dark crème de cacao
1½ ounces cream
1 teaspoon sugar

· Variations · For a POLAR BEAR, substitute ¾ ounce white crème de cacao for the dark.

To make a RUSSIAN CADILLAC, simply add ¾ ounce Galliano to the Polar Bear.

stimulating

· Caffeinated and fizzy drinks for a fun buzz ·

Mudslide

THIS DRINK HAS A WAY OF ENVELOPING YOU in a lusciously thick, creamy mudslide of perfectly decadent after-dinner flavors.

Shake the liquid ingredients vigorously with ice. Strain into a chilled cocktail glass. Sprinkle the top with cocoa powder or chocolate shavings.

1 ounce vodka
1 ounce Baileys Irish Cream
1 ounce Kahlúa
1 ounce cream
Unsweetened cocoa powder
  or chocolate shavings

· Variations · For a FROZEN MUDSLIDE, combine the ingredients in a blender with ½ cup crushed ice, and blend until smooth. Pour into a chilled wineglass.

Electric Leninade

THIS REFRESHINGLY BUBBLY ELABORATION on the 1930s classic
Blue Monday with the signature orange-flavored blue curaçao is
tarted up with sweet-and-sour.

Pour all of the liquid ingredients
except the 7-Up into an ice-filled
highball glass. Stir well. Top with
7-Up. Squeeze the lemon wedge
into the drink, and drop it in.

1½ ounces vodka
½ ounce blue curaçao
2 ounces sweet-and-sour
3 to 4 ounces chilled 7-Up
Lemon wedge

· Sweet-and-Sour · Citrus is an essential ingredient in many
drinks, and recipes frequently call for the classic sweet-and-sour
mixture that cuts to the chase and covers both your sweet
and citrus flavor needs. Makes 2¼ cups.

½ cup cooled simple syrup
  (page 40)
¾ cup fresh lime juice

¾ cup fresh lemon juice
¼ cup water

Pour all the ingredients into a clean glass jar, with a tight-fitting lid.
Close the lid tightly, and shake the contents together until well mixed.
Refrigerate until needed. It will keep for a week to 10 days.

Espresso Martini

FOR THOSE WHO JUST CAN'T GET ENOUGH CAFFEINE as the sun goes down, this rich, aromatic cocktail is guaranteed to fuel a night of energetic revelry. Hard-core coffee fans may want to try the Javanese Martini: Rim a cocktail glass with turbinado sugar, replace the Kahlúa with 1 ounce Tia Maria, omit the crème de cacao, and garnish with a lemon peel twist.

1½ ounces vodka, regular or vanilla-flavored

½ ounce dark crème de cacao

½ ounce Kahlúa

½ ounce espresso or strong coffee

3 espresso beans

Stir the liquid ingredients in a mixing glass with ice. Strain into a chilled cocktail glass. Garnish with the espresso beans.

Fig Leaf Fizz

THIS IS MY FAVORITE MIXOLOGICAL RESPONSE to the primordial urge for a fabulous flavor combination of orange and chocolate. If given a choice of orange liqueurs, my palate naturally gravitates toward the lush vanilla-orange tones of Tuaca, completed with a splash of a sparkling orange beverage such as Orangina or San Pellegrino to lighten things up.

Shake the vodka, Tuaca, and crème de cacao vigorously with ice. Strain into an ice-filled highball glass. Top with the sparkling tangerine beverage. Garnish with the orange slice and mint.

1½ ounces vodka

½ ounce Tuaca

½ ounce white crème de cacao

2 to 3 ounces sparkling tangerine or orange beverage

Orange slice

Fresh mint sprig

Index